Inspirations in Design

FOR THE CREATIVE QUILTER

EXERCISES TAKE YOU FROM STILL LIFE TO ART QUILT

  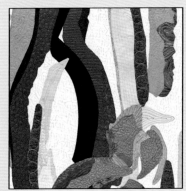

KATIE PASQUINI MASOPUST

C&T PUBLISHING

Text and Photography copyright © 2011 by Katie Pasquini Masopust

Photography and Artwork copyright © 2011 by C&T Publishing, Inc.

Publisher: Amy Marson

Creative Director: Gailen Runge

Acquisitions Editor: Susanne Woods

Editor: Lynn Koolish

Technical Editor: Sandy Peterson

Copyeditor: Randalyn Perkins

Proofreader: Wordfirm Inc.

Cover Designer: Kristen Yenche

Page Layout Artist: Kristen Yenche

Book Design Direction: Christina D. Jarumay

Production Coordinator: Jenny Leicester

Production Editor: Julia Cianci

Photography by Christina Carty-Francis and Diane Pedersen of C&T Publishing, Inc., unless otherwise noted

Published by C&T Publishing, Inc., P.O. Box 1456, Lafayette, CA 94549

Attention Teachers: C&T Publishing, Inc., encourages you to use this book as a text for teaching. Contact us at 800-284-1114 or www.ctpub.com for lesson plans and information about the C&T Creative Troupe.

We take great care to ensure that the information included in our products is accurate and presented in good faith, but no warranty is provided nor are results guaranteed. Having no control over the choices of materials or procedures used, neither the author nor C&T Publishing, Inc., shall have any liability to any person or entity with respect to any loss or damage caused directly or indirectly by the information contained in this book. For your convenience, we post an up-to-date listing of corrections on our website (www.ctpub.com). If a correction is not already noted, please contact our customer service department at ctinfo@ctpub.com or at P.O. Box 1456, Lafayette, CA 94549.

Trademark (™) and registered trademark (®) names are used throughout this book. Rather than use the symbols with every occurrence of a trademark or registered trademark name, we are using the names only in the editorial fashion and to the benefit of the owner, with no intention of infringement.

Library of Congress Cataloging-in-Publication Data

Pasquini Masopust, Katie, 1955-

Inspirations in Design for the Creative Quilter : Exercises Take You From Still Life to Art Quilt / Katie Pasquini Masopust.

pages cm

ISBN 978-1-60705-195-4 (soft cover)

1. Art quilts--Design. 2. Still-life in art. I. Title.

TT835.P3667 2011

746.46--dc22

                    2010048106

Printed in China

10 9 8 7 6 5 4 3 2 1

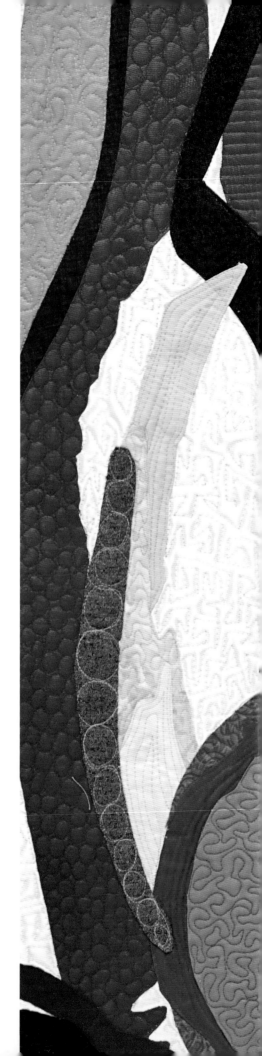

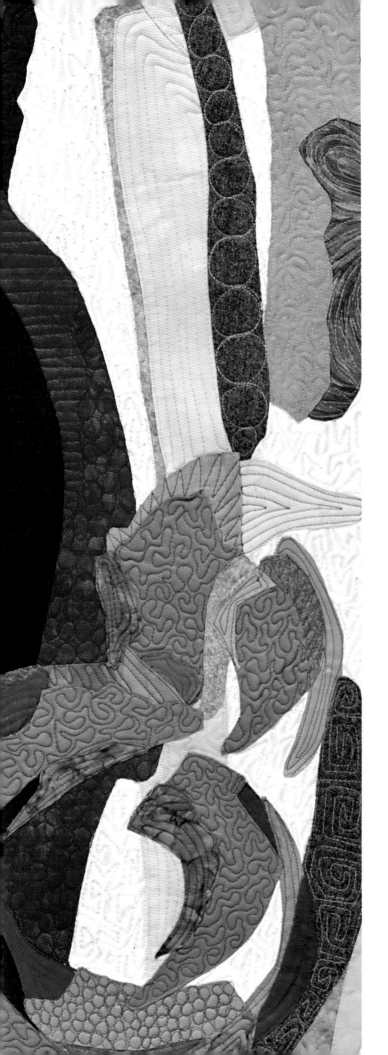

contents

PREFACE 5

INTRODUCTION 6

TOOLS AND SUPPLIES 7
• For Designing • For Construction • Still Life

COMPOSITION 9
• Set Up the Still Life • Compositions

COLOR 12
• Color Schemes • Value

EXPLORATIONS 18

Blind Contour Drawing—Slow

Blind Contour Drawing—Fast

Still Life with Shapes

Painting the Shadows

Tiled Still Life

Watercolor Painting

Positive/Negative

Repeat

Collage

Still Life from Photographs

FROM DESIGN TO FINISHED QUILT 70
• Materials   • Baste
• Plan the Colors   • Quilt
• Enlarge the Design   • Block
• Select Fabrics   • Make a Sleeve
• Cut Out the Fabrics   • Make a Label
• Assemble the Quilt Top   • Bind
• Machine Piece   • Document the Quilt
• Appliqué

ABOUT THE AUTHOR 79

DEDICATION

In Memoriam

To Bob Masopust Sr. for all of his years of support.

ACKNOWLEDGMENTS

I want to thank all of my students who helped me make this book so special by creating examples of the different explorations.

Thanks to my family for putting up with me through all my creative phases.

Thank you to my husband for all the wonderful computer gadgets he gives me to make writing a book more fun.

Thanks to Randi for editing my words and being my biggest fan on many levels.

preface

I AM A SELF-TAUGHT ARTIST. I started drawing and painting at a
very young age. There are seven siblings in my family; our parents encouraged
each of us to be individuals and gave us total support for our chosen avenues.
I wanted to be an artist. I took many classes in my youth to help develop my
talent and have always been creating in one form or another.

My sisters and I were taught to sew by making clothes for our dolls and later
for ourselves—we had very colorful wardrobes. In high school my electives
were chosen from the art courses: jewelry making, calligraphy, painting, and
drawing. I was even the set designer for most of our class productions, painting
huge sets and enjoying every moment of it. Then I got hooked on quilting and
made many traditional quilts before I met Michael James. He suggested I use my
knowledge of quilt construction and my talent for art to create art quilts. What
a turning point in my life! I focused on designing my own work. I also took art
classes for inspiration. I love to paint, and that has kept my quilts unique, as
many quilts are inspired by my paintings.

For this book, I took my cues from art classes and studies I have done in
the past. I thought it would be fun to work from still lifes, trying a variety of
approaches and transformations to create designs from which abstract quilts
could be made. I hope that you enjoy these designs and that they inspire you
to come up with your own ways of designing. Have fun.

introduction

This book includes ten chapters of explorations based on an all-white still life. I teach my Transforming the Still Life Class the same way that this book is organized and with the same established ground rules. Try the explorations first, following my rules, then think of ways to change my rules to make them your own, and continue on. I recommend you try each of the explorations to see what method of designing works best for you.

Each exploration is different from the next one. Not everyone will like all of the explorations; the job is to find ways of working that open your creative pathways and create excitement about what you are designing.

Follow this book from start to finish, and you will have several designs ready to be made into abstract art quilts when you are done. When you find a way of designing that excites you, I recommend that you start a series based on something in the original exercise, and think of new rules to add to make the design totally your own. Working in a series lets you explore many possibilities—the ideas that present themselves as you are working on one can be explored in subsequent pieces as the designs morph and mature.

tools and supplies

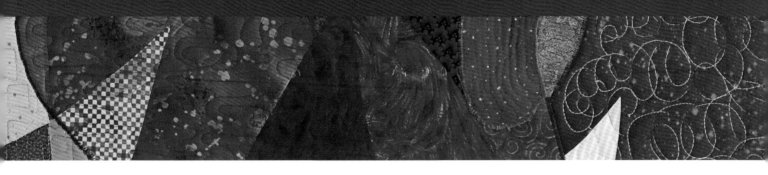

TOOLS AND SUPPLIES FOR DESIGNING

- **18″ × 24″ pad of drawing paper** for drawings

- **18″ × 24″ sheets of watercolor paper** for the painting exploration (page 42) and color studies (pages 13–16)

- **Tracing paper** for the repeat exploration (page 55) and for auditioning changes to the final drawings

- **Number 2 lead pencil and sharpener**

- **Several different sizes of flat brushes**

- **Pigma .01 black pen** for drawing the finished design onto acetate

- **Tombow black felt pen** (nontoxic) for filling in large areas in the tiling exploration (page 38)

- **Watercolor set for** color studies. Use an inexpensive set of cakes or student grade tubes—black, white, and the colors that you wish to work with from the color scheme you choose. With tubes you will need some type of palette; a plastic plate will do.

- **Plastic containers** to hold brushes and water

- **Paper scissors** for cutting and cropping designs

- **Black and white construction paper** for the positive/negative exploration (page 50)

- **Matte acetate** for the final drawing

- **Graphite paper** to transfer designs to watercolor paper to plan out colors

- **L-shaped cropping tool** for zooming in and finding the best part of the drawing or painting. A mat frame that is cut into two L's at the opposite corners does the job.

- **Masking tape** to edge your paintings

- **Table or floor easel** to hold the pad of drawing paper

- **Right-brain music** to listen to when you are drawing and painting to allow your right brain to play. Select music without words.

- **Spotlight or large flashlight** to create shadows for the paint-the-shadows exploration (page 34)

Tools and supplies for designing

TOOLS AND SUPPLIES FOR CONSTRUCTION

- **Fabrics in chosen color scheme** to make your quilt. Be sure to have a full value range of seven values from light to dark (page 17).

- **Poster board** for attaching the enlarged pattern to create piecing/appliqué templates (page 72)

- **Permanent spray adhesive** to glue the enlarged pattern to the poster board

- **Sulky Totally Stable Iron-on Tear-Away Stabilizer** for the foundation

- **Spray starch** to hold the fabric fold over the template for appliqué

- **Stiletto** to aid in turning the fabric edges over the template

- **Iron and ironing board** to turn fabric over the edges of the templates

- **Sewing machine with free-motion zigzag capability and darning foot**

- **Thin batting**

- **Spray-baste temporary adhesive** to make the quilt sandwich (optional: safety pins)

- **Threads** for quilting. Have multiple colors on hand.

- **Monofilament thread** for the invisible appliqué stitch (page 75)

- **Fabric pencils for marking** the turning line on the back of the fabric—red for marking on cool colors, green for marking on warm colors, white for marking on darks, and a number two lead pencil for marking on light colors

- **Quilting pins**

- **Gluestick**

- **Scissors** for cutting fabric and cardboard templates. Keep your good fabric shears sharp, and have another pair of scissors for paper and cardboard.

Tools and supplies for construction

STILL LIFE

You will be using white objects in the still life explorations. I have seen this done in many classrooms throughout my years of education. An all-white still life removes the distractions of colors and allows you to see the form and shadow more easily. This does not mean that the quilts designed from an all-white still life will be all white; color will be added after the drawing stage, and, in some of the exercises, you will draw with watercolors. To make your still life, gather objects that are all white: vases, cups, plates, silk flowers, yarn, teapots, shells, books, and so on. I like to use fruits in my still lifes, so I spray-paint plastic fruit and veggies white. This can also be done with an old book or anything you like the shape of that is not white. A student sent me two plastic pears he had painted white for me; I just love them and have used them in my still lifes for the book. (Thanks, Bill!)

All-white still life

composition

SET UP THE STILL LIFE

Set up a still life to use for the explorations that follow. It is fine to change the still life between each exploration, or keep the same setup to see the different possibilities with one still life. It is entirely up to you.

1. Fold a piece of poster board to make a backdrop for the still life.

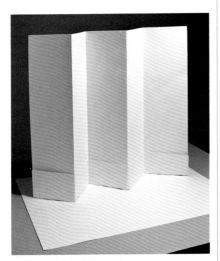

Fold poster board for backdrop.

2. Use white cloth to create a drape over part of the poster board and across the table.

Drape white cloth on poster board backdrop and table.

3. Place the still life objects against this backdrop. Think about the compositional elements (see Compositions, page 10) that you want to use.

Use all-white objects to create still life.

Setting up a good still life with a strong composition is half of the battle. Think about the way your eye moves around the still life, and choose different elements to be included: tall and short, soft edges (flowers) and hard edges (vases). Five or six elements should be sufficient. Have them overlap so it looks like things are grouped together. Consider the negative space (the spaces between the objects) and the space around the outside. Negative spaces should be as interesting as the objects. If there are large areas with nothing in them, think about draping the cloth to create folds that give interest to those empty areas.

COMPOSITIONS

Vertical composition: Dominant lines are running up and down.

Circular composition: Lines or shapes catch your eye and move it around the still life in a circular manner.

Horizontal composition: Dominant lines are horizontal.

Diagonal composition: Dominant lines are diagonal.

Radiating composition: Lines and/or shapes move outward from a central point.

Triangular composition: More objects at the bottom and one tall object create a visual triangle.

Symmetrical composition: The same on both sides of the middle

S composition: Moves your eye along in a curvy way

Asymmetrical composition: Each half is very different from the other.

color

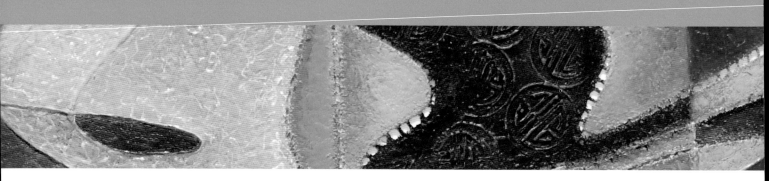

COLOR IS WHAT art quilts are all about, but color shouldn't be the first choice you make when designing a quilt. The subject matter, line, shape, and image are first, and then the design and composition. We all have so much beautiful fabric, and it is too easy to become seduced by the colors and textures. Save choosing colors and fabrics until after you've done the groundwork of creating a well-thought-out design. First, choose the subject, idea, or theme to translate into fabric. This can be a nonrepresentational drawing made up of lines or shapes, or an abstract painting, photograph, or cut-paper collage.

Play with these ideas, considering composition (the way the objects, lines, and or shapes are arranged within the frame of the drawing, page 10) and the way the eye travels through the piece.

When all those decisions are in place, it is time to choose the colors for the piece. There are many classic color schemes from which to choose. The first few exercises will be line drawings, so you won't worry about color until the design is chosen. For the painting exercises, you'll paint with the color scheme you are considering for the quilt.

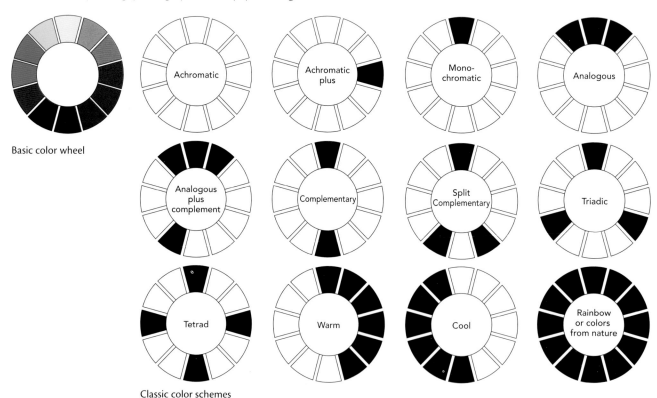

Basic color wheel

Classic color schemes

COLOR SCHEMES

The following are some classic color schemes from which to choose when you are doing the explorations.

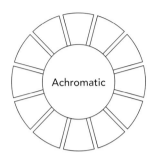

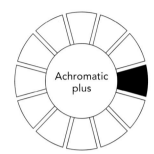

Achromatic: The absence of color. This can be white through shades of gray to black, or it can be black-and-white prints that are sorted into seven value steps (page 17).

Achromatic plus: A black-and-white color scheme with a little bit of color thrown in to create excitement

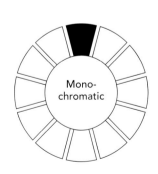

Monochromatic: One color with all of its values. This is a very elegant color scheme and one that is easy to work with when all seven values are used. Everything goes together because all parts are the same color.

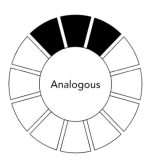

Analogous: Three colors that are next to each other on the color wheel. This is a very harmonious color scheme, as the colors have a bit of each other in them.

Analogous plus complement: Three colors that are next to each other on the color wheel plus one of their complements (see below). The complement adds a punch to this scheme.

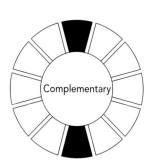

Complementary: One color plus the color opposite it on the color wheel. A complementary scheme is jazzy, as the colors are as far apart as they can be on the wheel. A full value range (page 17) is very important in this scheme to calm the vibration that is caused when middle-value opposites are placed together. The light and dark values help blend and calm this jazzy scheme.

Split Complementary: One color and the two colors on either side of its complement. These two colors soften the vibration that occurs when direct complements are used.

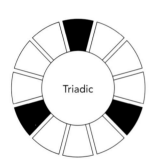

Triadic: Three colors separated by three colors; each contains none of the other colors, creating a lively interaction. The seven values (page 17) are equally important here.

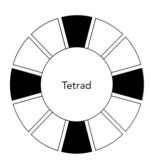

Tetrad: Any two colors and their complements. This is lively because of the use of two complements, but it can be toned down by using a full value range (page 17).

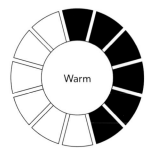 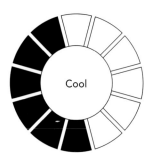

Warm: The six colors on the warm side of the wheel, which includes all the reds and oranges through to the yellows and results in a hot, fiery scheme

Cool: The six colors on the cool side of the wheel, which includes all the greens and blues through to the violets and results in a calm scheme

Rainbow: All the colors on the wheel are included. When used all together, it is important to organize them, or chaos will be created. Some organizational possibilities are to arrange them as they are found on the wheel, starting with any color and moving right or left around the wheel; to use complements together with warm for highlights (warm colors come forward) and cool for low lights or shades (cool colors recede); or to arrange the colors by value using the seven value steps (see Value, page 17).

VALUE

When you have finished the explorations and have chosen a design to work with, sort your fabrics into the classic color scheme you have chosen. Then sort your fabrics into seven value steps for a full value range.

Value 1 is the lightest of the color; very pale fabrics and white go in this step.

Value 2 is made up of fabrics with a bit more color in them.

Value 3 has more color in it. This is the place where pure yellow is placed.

Value 4 has even more color in it. This is the place where pure orange, red, blue, and green belong.

Value 5 is getting darker and is where pure violet is stationed.

Value 6 is dark.

Value 7 is where black and very dark values of the color are placed.

If you choose to use black-and-white prints, here is a helpful note on how to sort them.

Value 1 is white-on-white prints.

Value 2 is white background with a little bit of black print.

Value 3 is white background with more black print covering it.

Value 4 is in the middle and is prints, checks, stripes, and patterns where the amount of black and white is the same.

Value 5 is black background with a lot of white print on it.

Value 6 is black background with a little bit of white print.

Value 7 is black-on-black print.

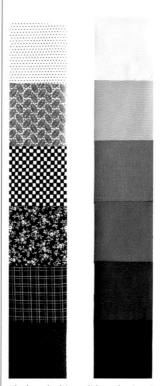

Black and white solids and prints in their appropriate value steps

Seven values of the primary colors

explorations

blind contour drawing —SLOW

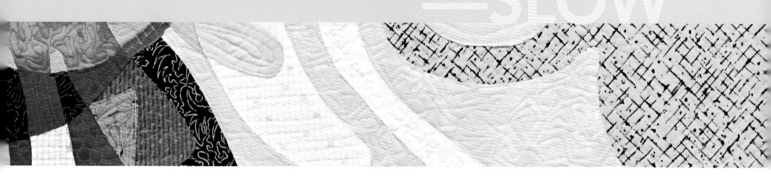

CONTOUR DRAWING is drawing with a solid line all the shapes and shadows and highlights of the objects; this does not include shading, just lines. Contour drawing is a common drawing exercise in most art classes. Blind contour drawing is drawing the objects without looking at the paper. This teaches you to really **see** the objects. Learning to see is the best way to learn to draw.

MATERIALS

- Easel
- Drawing pad
- Slow-paced instrumental music
- Pencil
- L-shaped cropping tool (page 7)
- Paper scissors
- Matte acetate or fairly clear tracing paper
- .01 black Pigma pen
- White paper
- Watercolor paper
- Graphite paper
- Masking tape
- Watercolors and brushes

INSTRUCTIONS

Contour Drawing

1. Set up your easel and drawing pad so that you can see your still life but not easily see your drawing surface.

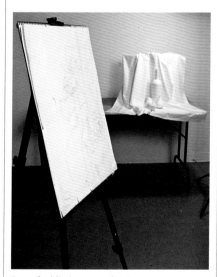

Setup for blind contour drawing

2. Play slow-paced instrumental music to create the right mood and to quiet the left brain—the left brain is the analytical side, and it will want to direct and criticize you. Try not to listen to the left brain's negative musings and enjoy the act of drawing.

3. Pick an edge of an object in the still life, and place the pencil on the paper in about the right spot. Now,

no longer look at the drawing surface as you slowly move your eye across the contours of the objects. Move the pencil at the same slow speed. Notice the edges and surfaces rather than the individual objects. Do not lift the pencil from the paper, and don't wonder if the drawing looks like the objects. You are learning to **see,** which is what drawing is all about. Your left brain may be telling you that you are wrong, that the pencil is not in the right place, and on and on. The music should help you access your right brain and try to quiet your left brain. You are making sketches and playing. The right brain really enjoys this part. Hold the pencil back from the point. This will help you relax and create a looser line. Spend about 20 minutes drawing the still life.

Blind contour drawing of still life

4. Look at your drawing. You will probably laugh the first few times you do this. Don't be judgmental. Put on more music. On a clean piece of paper repeat the exercise. I recommend you try this several times to get the hang of it. Remember to draw very slowly and discover the subtle nuances of all the surfaces.

5. When you have finished several drawings, hang them on the wall, and analyze them. Do you like the whole drawing or only a part of it? Generally there are areas within the drawing that you really like and areas that you don't. That is the reason for the L-shaped cropping tool!

6. Place the drawings on a table, and use the L-shaped cropping tool to isolate the best part of each of the drawings. Remember it is not important that it looks like a still life anymore. You are abstracting, transforming the still life. Isolate different sections that you like; it may be an interesting arrangement of lines or shapes. Analyze the composition. How does your eye travel across and through the picture plane in the area within the L-shaped cropping tool? Draw around the inside of the L-shaped cropping tool, and cut out that part as a design possibility. Several designs may be found in one drawing.

Crop to find best part of drawing.

1. Choose the best drawing to make into an art quilt.

2. Use matte acetate or a fairly clear tracing paper to trace and redraw your chosen design with a .01 black Pigma pen. This drawing should be very clear and very clean; every little smudge or line will show up later when enlarging the design to make templates for the quilt (see From Design to Finished Quilt, pages 70–78). Draw a frame around the perimeter of the design drawing on the acetate.

Trace design and frame on matte acetate.

3. Back the drawing with a piece of clean white paper.

Back acetate drawing with white paper.

4. Make a photocopy of the drawing to use for tracing the design onto watercolor paper. Don't enlarge the design at this point.

5. Trace the photocopied design 3 or more times onto watercolor paper using graphite paper.

Transfer design to watercolor paper with graphite paper.

Using Graphite Paper

Graphite paper is available in art supply stores. Here's how to use it:

1. Place the photocopy of the design right side up on a piece of water-color paper.

2. Place a piece of graphite paper under the photocopy.

3. Gently draw over the design to transfer it to the watercolor paper. Use very gentle pressure so the transferred lines are barely visible on the watercolor paper; otherwise they may muddy the paint.

6. Place masking tape around the edge of each drawing to keep a clean line around the painting.

Tape around edges.

7. Paint the design with watercolor paints, using several different color schemes (pages 13–16).

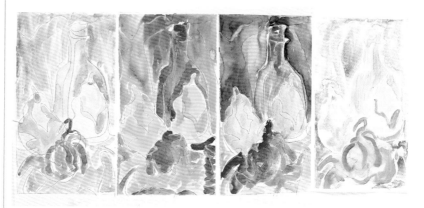

Four different color schemes

8. Hang the design options on the wall, and analyze the color schemes. Pick the one you like best.

9. Turn your design into a quilt by following the steps in From Design to Finished Quilt (pages 70–78).

Slow-contour drawing and cropping lines   Three painted color schemes

Slow Summer by Katie Pasquini Masopust, 23″ × 41″, 2008

Still Life with Pears by Katie Pasquini Masopust, 23″ × 40″, 2010

Student Works

Applelicious by Jessica Masopust Barber, 38″ × 30″, 2010

Chrysanthemum and Vase by Nancy Becker Reester, 20″ × 35″, 2009

There's a Giraffe in My Cave by Penny Haney, 22″ × 34″, 2010

Still Life by Mary Louise Gerek, 25″ × 36″, 2009

Two in the Bush by Tesi Vaara, 22″ × 32″, 2010

Abstract Still Life by Jeannie Palmer Moore, 28″ × 43″, 2009

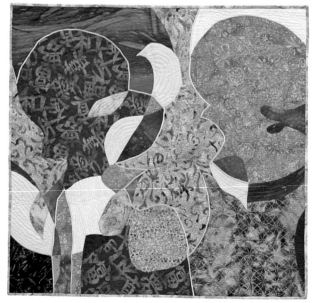

Aqua in Abstract by Alice Baird, 28″ × 27″, 2010

Eclipse by Bill Bowman, 17″ × 23″, 2009

blind contour drawing —FAST

FOR THIS BLIND CONTOUR drawing, you will draw fast. You should be familiar with the still life, as you drew it several times in the previous exploration. Put on fast-paced right-brain (instrumental) music and draw the still life quickly, moving to the beat of the music. This is a lot of fun.

MATERIALS

- Easel
- Drawing pad
- Fast-paced instrumental music
- Pencil
- L-shaped cropping tool (page 7)
- Paper scissors
- Matte acetate or fairly clear tracing paper
- .01 black Pigma pen
- White paper
- Watercolor or plain paper
- Graphite paper
- Masking tape
- Watercolors and brushes or colored pencils

INSTRUCTIONS
Contour Drawing

1. Set up your easel and drawing pad as you did for the Blind Contour Drawing–Slow exploration, so that you can see your still life but not easily see your drawing surface (page 19).

2. Choose instrumental or classical music that has a fast beat for motivation.

3. Decide on a spot to start, and place your pencil on the drawing pad. When the music begins, draw quickly. Stand back from the surface, and use your whole arm to draw the contours of the still life as fast as you can while still holding true to the shapes. This should only take a minute or two of music and drawing.

4. Look at your drawing. What do you think? Did you draw too slow and the drawing looks similar to the blind contour slow drawing? Or did you draw so fast that the drawing looks like a bunch of scribbles? Or are you pleased with it? Get a clean piece of paper and try this several more times.

Fast contour drawing

5. Put all the drawings up on a wall, and look at them for a while. Do you like the whole drawing? Often the whole drawing is great but would be a very ambitious quilt project, so it is often best to crop the design.

6. Place your drawings on the table, and use the L-shaped cropping tool to isolate the best part of the drawings. It is not important that it looks like a still life anymore. Make sure the composition is strong and there is a good variation of sizes within the shapes created by the intersecting lines. Notice how your eye moves around the surface. Are all areas interesting? Draw around the inside of the cropping tool, and cut out that part as a quilt possibility.

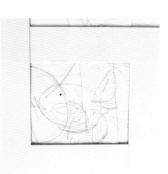
Crop to find the best part of drawing.

Create the Quilt

1. Choose the best design to make into an art quilt.

2. Follow Steps 2–4 (see Create the Quilt in Blind Contour Drawing—Slow, pages 20–21) to prepare the design.

3. Using graphite paper transfer the design from the photocopy 3 times to watercolor paper or plain paper, and place masking tape around the edge of each drawing to keep a clean line around the design. Paint using watercolors— or use colored pencils—to create several different color schemes or different placements of colors in the same color scheme.

Prepare design.

Three color possibilities made with colored pencil on copies of design

Dancing by Katie Pasquini Masopust, 36″ × 24″, 2009

4. Pick the color scheme you like the best. To turn your design into a quilt, follow the steps in From Design to Finished Quilt (pages 70–78).

Two color possibilities

Fast contour drawing and cropping lines

Ribbon of Life by Millicent Gillogly, 17″ × 51″, 2010

Pears Delight by Katie Pasquini Masopust, 27″ × 46″, 2010

Joy by Nancy Eisenhauer, 35″ × 42″, 2010

Red Swirls by Carolyn L. Olsen, 23½″ × 33″, 2011   *By Candlelight* by Jan Kopf, 22″ × 35″, 2009   *Think of Picasso* by Jane Munsell, 34″ × 49″, 2009

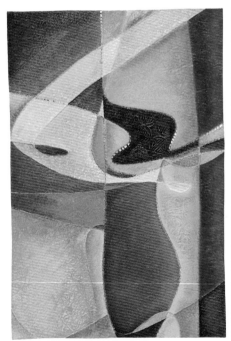

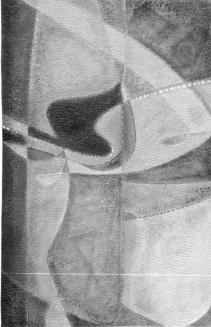

Pelvic Doorway by Carol Wiebe, a triptych of three quilts, each about 18¾″ × 26¼″, 2010

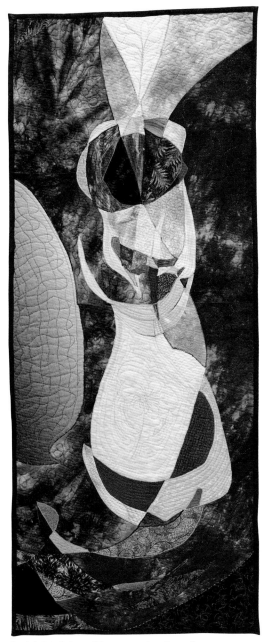

Genie's Bottle by Jackie L. Heupel, 20″ × 48″, 2010

Untitled by Valarie Maser-Flanagan, 22″ × 28″, 2009

Hot Times Deep in the Heart of Texas by Sara Sissenwein Norris, 45″ × 27″, 2009

still life with shapes

DRAW EACH OBJECT or part of this still life as a square or rectangle. The still life will give you suggestions on where to place the shapes. The squares and/or rectangles need to be parallel to the edge of the drawing paper—no diagonal placement in this exploration. Overlap squares to create dimension, and be sure to draw the background, the shadows, and the interesting shapes created by the still life.

MATERIALS

- Easel

- Drawing pad

- Slow-paced instrumental or classical music

- Pencil

- L-shaped cropping tool (page 7)

- Paper scissors

- Matte acetate or fairly clear tracing paper

- .01 black Pigma pen

- White paper

- Watercolor or plain paper

- Graphite paper

- Masking tape

- Watercolors and brushes or colored pencils

INSTRUCTIONS

1. Set up your easel and drawing pad so that you can see your still life and your drawing pad.

2. Play slow instrumental or classical music.

3. Draw the still life with the squares and/or rectangles. In your mind, see everything as squares or rectangles. Draw the background and the drape as squares as well. Squares can overlap to create transparency, or they can be on top to create opacity. A flower can be drawn as a square, with a square for the highlights and another square for the shadowed area. It is not necessary to draw each petal as a square, as this may get too complicated.

4. When you have finished, analyze the drawing. Do you like the whole thing? Is the negative space interesting, or do you need to add or erase some squares to make it so? Would cropping the drawing help?

5. Use the L-shaped cropping tool to see if you can find a strong composition using only part of the drawing. Draw around the inside of the cropping tool, and cut out this part for your design.

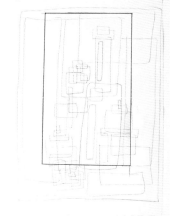

Still life drawing using only squares; cropping lines included

Create the Quilt

Follow Steps 2–8 in Blind Contour Drawing—Slow (pages 20–21) to reproduce, color the design, and create a quilt. Use either watercolor paints or colored pencils for your color schemes.

Often my students feel they are held back by my rules for this exploration—so make up your own rules using different shapes, such as circles, squares, and rectangles on the diagonal; triangles; a combination; or some other shape you like. Draw the still life using your new shapes and your new rules, and see what happens. Again, when you are done, either use the whole drawing or crop it to find an interesting part.

STUDENT WORKS WITH SQUARES

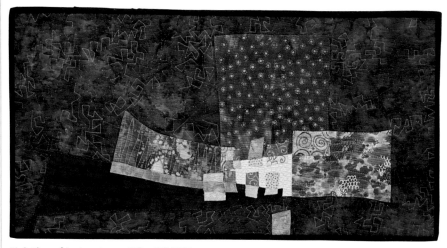

Pink Flower[2] by Jory Agate, 12″ × 20″, 2009

I knew I wanted to do a monochromatic yellow scheme, so I just added value placements to the drawing.

Yellow Still Life by Katie Pasquini Masopust, 17″ × 32″, 2010

All That Jazz
by Priscilla J. Smith, 34″ × 48″, 2008

Balance & Counterbalance
by Diane Morrow, 27″ × 36″, 2009

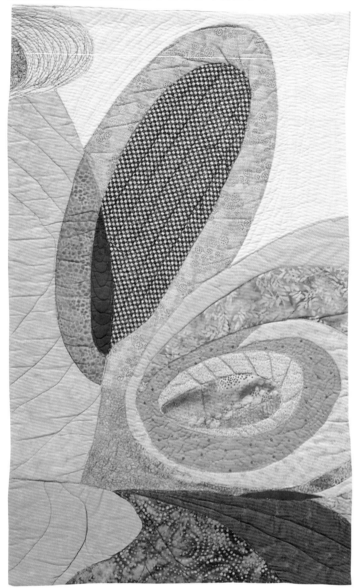

Sara's Study by Barbara Bowman, 23″ × 24″, 2009

Soft Landing by Jeanette Davis, 21″ × 34″, 2009

Teapot Jazz I by Amy Witherow, 33½″ × 35½″, 2009

Three Sides to Every Story by Kathy R. Nurge, 22″ × 35″, 2010

Happy! by Donna Dynes, 27¼″ × 32½″, 2010

Very Berry Still by Pamela Braswell, 24″ × 27¾″, 2011

Floating Aspens by Barb Caldwell, 36″ × 36″, 2010

painting the shadows

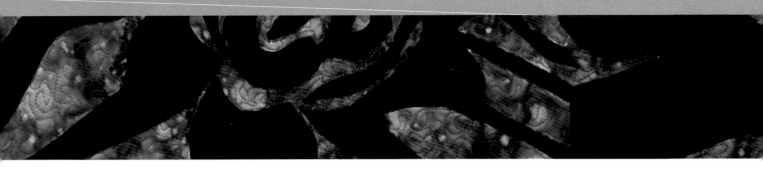

PAINTING THE SHADOWS is an effective way to create an abstract design. In this exploration, point a spotlight or flashlight at the still life to create dramatic shadows; then paint the shadows, not the objects that create them.

MATERIALS

- Easel
- Drawing pad
- Slow-paced instrumental music
- Spotlight or strong flashlight
- Pencil
- Black watercolor paint
- ½" flat paintbrush
- L-shaped cropping tool (page 7)
- Matte acetate or fairly clear tracing paper
- .01 black Pigma pen
- White paper
- Watercolor or plain paper
- Graphite paper
- Masking tape
- Watercolors and brushes or colored pencils

INSTRUCTIONS

1. Set up your easel and drawing pad so that you can see your still life and your drawing pad.

2. Set the spotlight or flashlight to create intense shadows on your still life and the backdrop. Turn the overhead lights in the room down low. Do you like what you see? If not, move the light around until you have dramatic shadows.

3. Turn the lights up, and with a pencil, draw the placement of the objects. This is to be a very simple drawing so you know where on the paper all the objects are in relation to one another; do not include too much detail.

Still life with spotlight

4. Turn the overhead lights down, and paint the shadows with black watercolor paint. Everything should be black, not shades of gray. I have found that the successful paintings have more black than white paper showing. Keep painting the shadows; if any look gray, paint them black so there is a strong contrast of black and white.

5. Analyze your painting. Are there equal amounts of black areas and white areas? If so, paint more black areas. You are the artist; if there is no black area where you need it in the still life, you can paint it in on your painting. Are the shapes well-defined or a little sketchy? Clarify the strokes so they are black shapes.

6. Use the L-shaped cropping tool, and see if you can isolate the best part of the painting.

7. Use matte acetate or a fairly clear tracing paper to redraw your design using a .01 black Pigma pen. This drawing should be very clear and very clean; every little smudge or line will show up in the enlargement used to make the quilt. Draw a frame around the perimeter of the design, drawing on the acetate. Back this drawing with a piece of clean white paper.

8. If you are going to make a black-and-white quilt, there is no need to create a color placement painting. If you are considering creating the quilt in a different color scheme, make a photocopy of your acetate drawing to use for tracing the design onto watercolor paper with graphite paper, and make at least 3 different paintings with the possible color schemes (pages 12–16) you want to use. Pick the best color scheme.

9. To turn your design into a quilt, follow the steps in From Design to Finished Quilt (pages 70–78).

Shadow painting

Cropped section

Flowers by Katie Pasquini Masopust, 32″ × 25″, 2009

Shadow painting   Cropped section

Sleeping Pears by Katie Pasquini Masopust, 19″ × 12″, 2010

Shadow painting

Tea Party by Katie Pasquini Masopust, 20″ × 24″, 2010

STUDENT WORKS

Shadows by Donna Moog, 32″ × 50″, 2010

My Achromatic Apple by Nancy Greaves Sinise, 33½″ × 32″, 2011

tiled still life

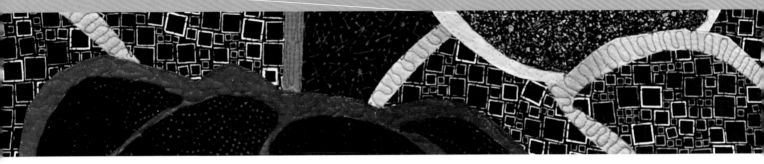

 T HIS EXPLORATION will create a cartoonish design by simplifying the shapes. By
filling in the shapes and leaving a border around each shape, you'll have a design that
looks like tiles with grout or mortar between them.

MATERIALS

- Easel

- Drawing pad

- Slow-paced instrumental music

- Tombow black felt pen

- L-shaped cropping tool (page 7)

- Paper scissors

- Matte acetate or fairly clear
  tracing paper

- .01 black Pigma pen

- White paper

- Watercolor or plain paper

- Graphite paper

- Masking tape

- Watercolors and brushes or colored
  pencils

INSTRUCTIONS

1. Set up the easel and the drawing pad so you can see the pad and the still life.

2. Make 4 windows on the drawing pad so you can make 4 different drawings
of the same still life.

Four windows

3. Draw the still life in the first window with the Tombow pen, simplifying the shapes. At this point you may see that there are too many objects in the still life for the little window.

4. Simplify the still life by removing some of the objects. Draw the still life again in the second window.

5. Analyze the 2 drawings. Do you like them? If not, why not? Notice the way your eye travels around the drawing. Are all areas interesting? Does your drawing seem too stiff? That could be because you are looking at your drawing more than at the still life, and you have lost the looseness of the blind contour drawing.

Two drawings for tiling

6. Draw the still life in the third window, looking at the still life 80% of the time and at the paper only 20% of the time.

7. Draw the still life one more time in the fourth window. Choose the one you like the best. If you don't like any of them, you can start over, but hang on a bit. The next step changes everything.

Note

The purpose of drawing the same still life four times is to familiarize yourself with the shapes. Each drawing will be a little different. Small changes happen each time you draw it.

8. Fill in all the shapes with the black pen, leaving a bit of white along the edges.

Fill in the tiles.

9. Use matte acetate or a fairly clear tracing paper to redraw your design using a .01 black Pigma pen, tracing the edges of the black shapes. This drawing should be very clear and very clean. Every little smudge or line will show up in the enlargement used to make the quilt. Draw a frame around the perimeter of the design drawing on the acetate. Back this drawing with a piece of clean white paper.

10. If you are going to make a black-and-white quilt, there is no need to create a color placement painting. If you are considering creating the quilt in a different color scheme, make a photocopy of your acetate drawing to use for tracing the design onto watercolor paper or plain paper with graphite paper, and make at least 3 different paintings with the possible color schemes you want to use. Pick the best color scheme.

11. To turn your design into a quilt, follow the steps in From Design to Finished Quilt (pages 70–78).

Drawing ready for enlargement

Three drawings of pear still life

Reading Time by Katie Pasquini Masopust, 17″ × 22″, 2009

Wine and Roses by Katie Pasquini Masopust, 14″ × 32″, 2010

STUDENT WORKS

Still Life of Father Time by Terre Walker, 21″ × 29″, 2009

Still Life à la Katie by Catherine Beard, 35″ × 49″, 2007

Summer Song by Barbara Bowman, 33½″ × 41″, 2009

Apple Wine: An Abstract by Michele Whetstone, 21″ × 26″, 2011

watercolor painting

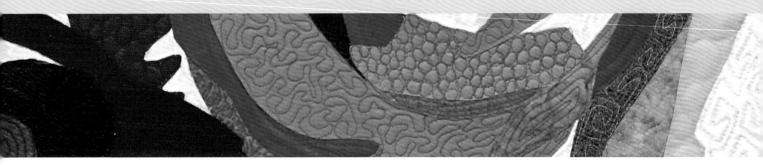

W ATERCOLOR PAINTS are great for creating abstract paintings—they run and blend and bleed into each other, creating uncontrolled and wonderful designs. There are two different parts to this exploration, and since the paintings need to dry at certain points, you will paint two paintings at once, moving back and forth between them, allowing them to dry. Try not to paint the still life realistically; use the arrangement of the objects to suggest where the paint strokes should be applied. Using your chosen color scheme, paint loosely, and allow the paint to do its magic. Be sure to leave the highlights unpainted, because you can't get the white paper back.

MATERIALS

- Watercolor paper
- Upbeat instrumental music
- Watercolor paints in the color scheme that you choose
- 1″ flat brush
- L-shaped cropping tool (page 7)
- Paper scissors
- Matte acetate or fairly clear tracing paper
- .01 black Pigma pen
- White paper
- Graphite paper

INSTRUCTIONS

1. Set the drawing pad on a flat surface so you can see the pad and the still life.

2. Fold the watercolor paper in half, so you can create the 2 paintings side by side, moving from one to the other.

3. On one half of the watercolor paper, paint the still life using only *straight* lines that are parallel to the edges of the paper (horizontal and vertical lines only). Use the flat of the brush to make wide strokes and the edge of the brush to make thin lines. Put one layer down first, and while that layer is drying, work on the drawing on the other half of the watercolor paper.

4. For the second painting, use the same brush, but paint the still life with flowing organic lines. (Organic lines are the opposite of the straight lines used for the first painting. They are curved and flowing.) Put a layer down, and while that is drying, return to the first drawing.

5. Add some dark strokes to represent the shadows and the darker areas of the still life.

6. While the first painting dries, do the same to the second, organic painting, adding dark strokes for the shadows and darker areas.

7. To the first painting, add some very light washes by adding more water to the watercolor paint and brushing some light strokes to help blend all the paint that is already there. Notice where you have a lot of white paper showing, and brush the light washes through parts of these areas.

8. Add some light strokes to the second painting.

9. When everything is dry, hang the paintings up, and analyze them. Do you like the whole painting? Or do you need to get your L-shaped cropping tool and find a great little abstract section of the whole?

10. Draw around the L-shaped cropping tool, and cut out this section. Look for other possibilities, and cut these out as well. Hang them on the wall to analyze and find the best design.

11. On matte acetate draw around all the paint strokes with a .01 black Pigma pen. Be sure to draw around the areas created by bleeding or overlapping of the paint. Draw a frame around the perimeter of the design drawing on the acetate. This drawing will be used to enlarge the design to make the quilt.

12. To turn your design into a quilt, follow the steps in From Design to Finished Quilt (pages 70–78).

Still life

Cropped line painting

Acetate drawing of line painting

Grid by Katie Pasquini Masopust, 19″ × 32″, 2010

Cropped organic painting

Acetate drawing of organic painting

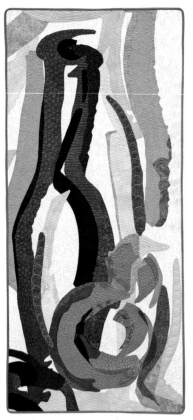

Friends by Katie Pasquini Masopust, 19″ × 40″, 2010

Painting of a rose with straight lines

Mercado by Katie Pasquini Masopust, 40″ × 60″, 2006, from the Hendricks Collection

Touching the Edge by Paulette Landers, 36″ × 37″, 2010

An Exercise in the Still Life by Leigh Layton, 30″ × 36″, 2010

Bouncing Off Lilies by Barbara Jean Kelly LaLiberte, 33¼″ × 43¾″, 2010

Brush Strokes by Beverly Fine, 28″ × 44″, 2010

Joie de Vivre by Shandra S. Belknap, 51½″ × 56″, 2010

Brush Strokes by Debbie Ross, 34″ × 39″, 2011

Brush Strokes by Carol Newhart, 29″ × 37″, 2011

Ties That Bind by Elaine Cominos Hickey, 28″ × 64″, 2007

January Still Life by Serena Brooks, 31¼″ × 40¾″, 2010

Heaven's Tears by Bill Bowman, 31¾″ × 29″, 2010

Orange Variation I by Judy Gaynes Sebastian, 23½″ × 37″, 2008

Imagination by Ann B. Graf, 29″ × 44″, 2008

Weird Flower by Diane H. Sharp, 50″ × 50″, 2010

Wisteria by Jeanne Muhl, 22″ × 45″, 2010

Joyful Surge by Carol F. Hazen, 37½″ × 26″, 2010

Water Color Series #3 by Linda J. Gallagher, 17″ × 69″, 2008

positive/negative

POSITIVE/NEGATIVE is about transposing values to create a checkerboard effect within the still life. Think of the old days when you got your film back and the negatives had the values reversed; what was black in reality was white on the film, and what was white or light was black and dark on the film. Imagine that you could take the picture and the negative film, cut them up, and rearrange them to create a high-contrast design.

MATERIALS

- Black and white construction paper
- Slow-paced instrumental music
- Scissors
- Gluestick
- Pencil
- L-shaped cropping tool (page 7)
- Matte acetate or fairly clear tracing paper
- .01 black Pigma pen
- White paper
- Watercolor paper
- Graphite paper
- Masking tape
- Watercolors and brushes

INSTRUCTIONS

1. Cut black and white construction paper to create your version of positive/negative using the still life.

2. Glue the pieces in place on a background of white or black or a combination of both.

There are several ways to go about doing the positive /negative. I don't like to give too much guidance, because I enjoy seeing where each individual takes this exercise. I have found that positive/negative means different things to different people. I encourage you to not read any further and to see where you go with this on your own; then try some of my options.

Option 1

1. Create a black-and-white background based on the folds in the poster board and the drape of the cloth in the still life.

Layer black and white paper to cut 1 of each.

Black and white shapes arranged to make a pieced background

2. Freehand cut shapes that are simplified versions of the objects in the still life. To do this, place the sheets of black and white construction paper together, and cut 2 of each shape.

3. Place the white shapes on the background, and draw where the lines of the pieced background cross the shapes. Place the black construction paper shape under the white shape with the drawn lines on it. Cut along the drawn lines, making 2 sets of 1 shape.

Draw background lines on shape.

4. Place the pieces in order on top of the background, replacing the black or white values. Where the object crosses the black background, place the white shape, and where the object crosses the white background, place the black shape. Continue until the whole shape is formed, creating a checkerboard effect. Glue the pieces in place.

Place shapes on background.

5. Analyze the design for compositional content.

6. Crop if needed using the L-shaped cropping tool.

7. Use matte acetate or a fairly clear tracing paper to redraw your design with a .01 black Pigma pen. This drawing should be very clear and very clean; every little smudge or line will show up in the enlargement used to make the quilt. Draw a frame around the perimeter of the design drawing on the acetate. Back this drawing with a piece of clean white paper.

8. If you are going to make a black-and-white quilt, there is no need to create a color placement painting. If you are considering creating the quilt in a different color scheme, make a photocopy of your acetate drawing to use for tracing the design onto watercolor paper with graphite paper, and make at least 3 different paintings with the possible color schemes you want to use. Choose the best color scheme.

9. To turn your design into a quilt, follow the steps in From Design to Finished Quilt (pages 70–78).

Option 2

1. Freehand cut still life shapes by placing a black piece and a white piece of construction paper together, folding the sheets in half, and cutting out the shapes.

2. Cut the sets of shapes in half along the fold, and then reconstruct them using both black and white pieces.

Alternate black and white halves.

3. Arrange the shapes to cover the background, and glue them in place.

4. Analyze the design for compositional content.

5. Crop if needed using the L-shaped cropping tool.

Completed design

6. Follow Steps 7–9 in Option 1 (page 51) to make your quilt.

Positive/negative design

Penguin Pears by Katie Pasquini Masopust, 18″ × 23″, 2010

I'm Positive...It's Not Negative by Ginger Cullins, 43″ × 29″, 2010

Pots of the Palisades by Vicki L. Bass, 24″ × 36″, 2009

Blushing Monochrome by Cherrie Hampton, 21″ × 27″, 2010

Miracles of Photosynthesis at Monterey Bay by Kerry Britton, 32″ × 27″, 2010

Mirrored Mind by Wendy F. Strumwasser, 24″ × 34″, 2010

Positive-Negative Still Life by Ina Block, 34″ × 41″, 2010

Black and White Still Life by Nancy Eisenhauer, 24″ × 18″, 2010

Double Tea by Amy Witherow, 29″ × 37″, 2010

repeat

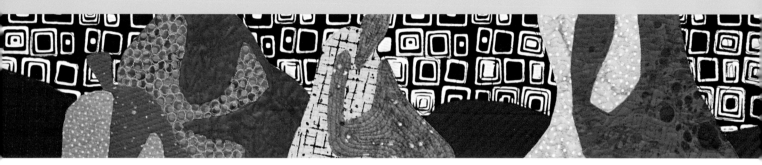

R EPEAT PATTERNS are the cornerstones of quiltmaking. The mind likes to see
things in repeat because it sets up a pattern and creates rhythm. For this exploration, draw the still life in two different sizes; then combine the two drawings to create the
composition.

MATERIALS

- Easel
- Drawing paper
- Upbeat instrumental music
- Tracing paper
- Pencil
- L-shaped cropping tool (page 7)
- Paper scissors
- Matte acetate or fairly clear tracing paper
- .01 black Pigma pen
- White paper
- Watercolor or plain paper
- Graphite paper
- Masking tape
- Watercolors and brushes or colored pencils

INSTRUCTIONS

1. Set up the easel and the drawing pad so you can see the pad and the still life.

2. Begin by drawing a simplified version of your still life on drawing paper. This will be a large drawing, so fill the whole paper. Remember, draw-ings turn out better when you look at the still life 80% of the time and look at the paper only 20% of the time. You may wish to draw without looking at the paper at all—this creates a more free-form and abstract rendition of the still life.

Draw large version of still life on drawing paper.

3. Draw the same still life, about half the size of the first drawing, on a piece of tracing paper that is bigger than your larger drawing.

Draw small version of still life on tracing paper.

4. Place the tracing paper drawing on top of the larger drawing, and find a good placement for it. Notice how the repeat objects create a rhythm.

5. Trace the larger drawing onto the tracing paper around the little drawing. Do not draw the big drawing where it is behind the little drawing.

Combine drawings.

6. Analyze the combined drawing. Do you like the whole thing, or would it benefit from cropping?

7. Crop the design using the L-shaped cropping tool if needed.

8. Use matte acetate or a fairly clear tracing paper to trace and redraw your design with a .01 black Pigma pen. This drawing should be very clear and very clean; every little smudge or line will show up in the enlargement used to make the quilt. Draw a frame around the perimeter of the drawing on the acetate. Back this drawing with a piece of clean white paper.

9. Make a copy of the drawing, and transfer it to watercolor or drawing paper using graphite paper. Choose color placement using water-colors or colored pencils. Pick the best color scheme.

Painted still life repeat

10. To turn your design into a quilt, follow the steps in From Design to Finished Quilt (pages 70–78).

Bouquet of Flowers by Katie Pasquini Masopust, 23″ × 24″, 2010

Large drawing of pears and bottle

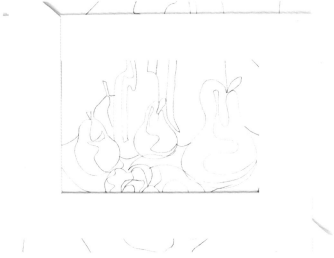

Cropped image

Small drawing of pears and bottle

Drawing simplified by leaving out bottles

Combined drawings

Jazzy Pears by Katie Pasquini Masopust, 25″ × 16″, 2010

Cheshire Petals by Natalia Masopust, 22″ × 33″, 2010

Sunny Thoughts by Judy Steward, 35″ × 31″, 2010

Two Loopy Flowers by Diane H. Sharp, 15½″ × 15″, 2009

Alegre 2009 by Lynn Moodie Elkinton, 18″ × 33″, 2010

Dream Lily by Beverly H. Hammack, 26″ × 16″, 2010

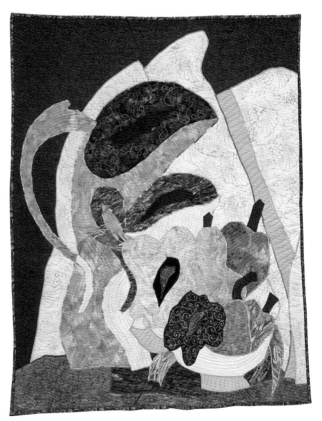

Distorted Repeat by Mary E. Price (Libby), 24″ × 36″, 2011

collage

OFTEN LEFTOVERS will make great designs. Look through all the left-over parts of all the explorations, the parts that remain after you cropped and cut out the section that you liked. See if they have anything in common and can be collaged together to create a whole design.

MATERIALS

- Watercolor paintings and line drawings
- White paper
- Upbeat instrumental music
- Rotary cutter, ruler, and mat
- Tape
- L-shaped cropping tool (page 7)
- Matte acetate or fairly clear tracing paper
- .01 black Pigma pen
- White paper

INSTRUCTIONS

Option 1: Collage

1. Look over the leftover bits from the exercises in the previous chapters. Cut out any of the shapes or arrangements of line that are interesting.

2. Place the chosen shapes on a piece of white paper (for the backing), and play with the composition.

3. Analyze the collage, and see if you like the whole thing or if it needs to be cropped to create a stronger composition.

4. Crop with the L-shaped cropping tool.

5. Use matte acetate or a fairly clear tracing paper to redraw your design with a .01 black Pigma pen. This drawing should be very clear and very clean; every little smudge or line will show up in the enlargement used to make the quilt. Draw a frame around the perimeter of the drawing. Back this drawing with a piece of clean white paper.

6. Use graphite paper to transfer the design to watercolor paper, and experiment with a color scheme you would like to use. Pick the best color scheme.

7. To turn your design into a quilt, follow the steps in From Design to Finished Quilt (pages 70–78).

Collaged pieces by Jane Barrows Broaddus

Daikon Figure It Out by Jane Barrows Broaddus, 20″ × 40″, 2009

A Whim My Way by Pam Dziewiontkowski, 23″ × 33″, 2010

The Path by Elizabeth Warner, 28" × 28½", 2010

Still Life with Teapot by Jane Stricker, 24" × 34", 2010

Sunshine and Moonshadows by Alison Chandler-Johnson,
23" × 35", 2011

Option 2: Grid Construction

1. Take the leftover bits from the previous painting explorations, and cut them into 2″ or 3″ squares.

2. Arrange the squares to make a pleasing composition. The squares can be placed together so there is no sashing; or you may wish to leave space to separate them, as sashing would. Take pictures of both designs to see which you like best. You can even cut them into different sizes and work them together. You may want to combine the painted straight lines with the organic paint lines, or try them on their own; sometimes less is more.

3. Follow Steps 3–6 from Option 1 (page 60) to make your design.

4. To turn your design into a quilt, follow the steps in From Design to Finished Quilt (pages 70–78).

Painting of still life

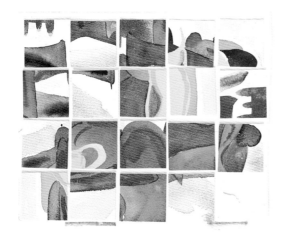

Cut-up and rearranged painting

Acetate drawing of squares

Deep Down and High Above by Katie Pasquini Masopust, 21″ × 32″, 2009

Squares and rectangles arranged to make a composition

Layers by Katie Pasquini Masopust, 46″ × 26″, 2010

STUDENT WORKS

Fractured Reflections by Eileen Keane, 33″ × 27″, 2010

Flowering Brushstrokes by Jan Sheets, 45″ × 35″, 2010

still life from PHOTOGRAPHS

I HAVE CREATED several still lifes during my art quiltmaking career. I accomplished these at different stages of my series work, and I have shown them in the books about those series (see About the Author, page 79). They fit well here, so I am including them again. The photos were transformed by changing the color, adding color, or arranging them in a manner different from the original photo.

MATERIALS

- Photographs of still life
- L-shaped cropping tool (page 7)
- Matte acetate
- .01 black Pigma pen
- Watercolor or drawing paper
- Graphite paper
- Watercolors or colored pencils

INSTRUCTIONS

1. Take photographs of your still life, and select your favorite picture. Be sure you analyze it for design and strength of composition.

2. Crop, if needed, using the L-shaped cropping tool.

3. Enlarge the photo to at least 8½" × 11".

4. Place a piece of matte acetate on top of the photo, and draw all the shapes and value changes with a .01 black Pigma pen for your design. Draw a frame around the perimeter of the design drawing on the acetate.

5. If you choose to change the color dramatically, I suggest you transfer the drawing to watercolor or drawing paper using graphite paper, and color in the shapes using watercolors or colored pencils. Choose the best color scheme.

6. To turn your design into a quilt, follow the steps in From Design to Finished Quilt (pages 70–78).

Setup for *Glass Carafes*. This was originally done for my Ghost Layers and Color Wash series; there is a ghost of two repeats of the round stopper from one of the carafes.

Glass Carafes by Katie Pasquini Masopust, 39″ × 57″, 1999

Photo by Hawthorne Studio

Glass Carafes with Checks by Katie Pasquini Masopust, 30″ × 36″, 1999, from the collection of Christa Manning. *Glass Carafes with Checks* is from the Ghost Layers and Color Wash series.

Photo by Hawthorne Studio

Photograph of glasses and the cropping line

Acetate drawing of glasses

Cheers by Katie Pasquini Masopust, 45″ × 45″, 2007

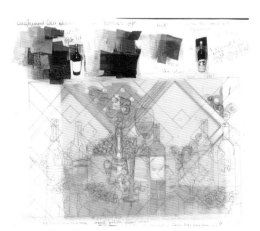

Photograph, acetate drawing, and color samples

Wine Tasting by Katie Pasquini Masopust, 80″ × 60″, 2005

Photo by Hawthorne Studio

Cut Crystal by Katie Pasquini Masopust, 55" × 85", 2001,
from the collection of Joan and Bob Becktal

Photo by Hawthorne Studio

Blue Bird by Natalia Masopust, 26" × 50", 2011

from design
TO FINISHED QUILT

From Design to Pattern

YOU HAVE analyzed several designs and made improvements in them, and now it is time to create a pattern that will enable you to successfully make the quilt.

MATERIALS

- White paper
- Proportion scale
- Masking tape
- Poster board
- Spray adhesive
- Matte acetate with drawn design
- .01 Micron Pigma pen

INSTRUCTIONS

Plan the Colors

1. Choose the design you want to make into a quilt, and make sure you have a clean acetate drawing (created earlier in one of the exploration sections).

2. If you haven't already planned the colors, use graphite paper to transfer the design to watercolor paper, and make at least 3 different paintings with the possible color schemes you want to use. Choose the color scheme that feels right.

Three paintings for *Slow Summer* (page 22)

Enlarging Your Design

Using a proportional scale is an easy way to figure out what percentage to enlarge a drawing. There are two wheels on the proportional scale. The small wheel relates to the size of the small drawing. The large wheel relates to the size of the large quilt. The tool makes it easy. Just follow these steps:

1. Measure one side of the drawing. Let's say it is 8". Find 8" on the small wheel, and hold it with your finger.

2. How long do you want that side of your quilt to be? Let's say you want it to be 35". Roll the small wheel around until the 8" mark is below the 35" mark on the large wheel.

3. The wheel is set. Look into the window on the small wheel where it says, "percentage of original size." The arrow points to 440%. That is the percentage of enlargement. Ask the copy shop to set the copier to 440% to get the proper size.

4. You can also check to see what the other dimension of your quilt will be. Measure the other dimension of the drawing. Let's say the drawing is 8" × 12". Without moving the wheel, find 12" on the small wheel, and look to see what the measurement is on the large wheel. At 440%, the other dimension of your quilt will be 53". If you enlarge your 8" × 12" drawing by 440%, your quilt will be 35" × 53".

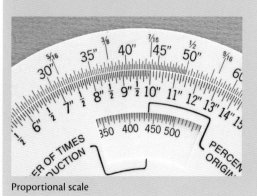
Proportional scale

If you don't have access to a proportional scale, you can figure the percentage of enlargement mathematically by dividing the size you want the quilt to be by the size of the drawing and then multiplying that number by 100.

Enlarge the Design

1. Cut the acetate ½" larger than the drawn frame on the final matte acetate drawing. Tape a piece of white paper to the back of the acetate drawing. The white paper ensures that none of the shadows and lines from the copy machine will be picked up when the design is copied.

Prepare acetate for enlarging.

2. Decide what size you want the quilt to be. There are many reasons to choose a particular size. Is there a spot on your wall that you want the quilt to fit? Is there a size requirement for a show you would like to enter? If your design contains many small shapes, you may need to make a large quilt in order to be successful, as larger pieces are much easier to work with. Once you have determined the dimensions of the quilt, use a proportional scale to calculate the percentage the design will need to be enlarged.

3. Take the acetate line drawing, taped to a piece of clean white paper, to a copy shop, and have three enlarged copies made. Most larger copy shops have machines that can make copies up to 36″ wide. If your design will be larger than 36″, it will be enlarged in 36″-wide strips that can be taped together (on the back) to create the whole.

Copy #1

One of the enlarged copies will be used to create templates for the appliqué pieces. The following is the process:

1. With masking tape, tape together poster board to create a piece that is the same size or larger than the copy. Tape the full length of the joint. Leave the taped side up.

2. Use spray adhesive to adhere the copy to the poster board. The tape (if you used it) is now on the inside, between the poster board and the pattern. (This will be important later if you use an iron to turn the edges. The iron won't touch the tape because it is between the poster board and the pattern.)

3. Cut out the shapes as needed when cutting and turning the fabrics.

Copy #2

The second enlarged copy will be used as a map for the placement of the pieces as they are cut out.

Staple or pin this copy to your design wall. The design wall should be made of something that will be easy to pin or staple to, such as cork or Celotex (sometimes known as builder's board).

Copy #3

The third enlarged copy has multiple uses. One is for tracing the pattern onto stabilizer for appliqué (page 74). It also serves as a fail-safe in case you lose templates and need to make more, or if you need to look at something to see where your pieces go. This process is like putting together a jigsaw puzzle. Consider the third copy the puzzle box top that you refer to during construction.

Select Fabrics

Sort your fabrics into the seven value steps as explained on page 17. Arrange the fabrics so you can see all the colors and values.

You now have the patterns, guides, and fabrics you need to begin the quilt.

Construction

Y OU HAVE your pattern and are ready to determine the best way to construct the quilt. If your pattern is based on straight lines, the quilt can be constructed with machine piecing (page 74). If your pattern has curves or irregular shapes, the construction can be done with my invisible-stitch appliqué technique (page 75).

MATERIALS

- Pattern

- Paper scissors

- Fabric scissors

- Fabric-marking pencils
  (I use Prismacolor colored pencils.)

- Quilting pins

- Gluestick

- Stabilizer for appliqué
  (I recommend Sulky Totally Stable.)

- Spray starch

- Stiletto

- Sewing machine with straight sewing foot and darning foot

- Thread for piecing and quilting

- Monofilament thread

- Optional: basting spray or safety pins for basting

INSTRUCTIONS

Cut Out the Fabrics

1. Place the fabric wrong side up, and place the pattern template wrong side up on top of it. Draw around the template with a fabric-marking pencil.

Place template upside down on fabric.

2. Cut the fabric ¼" beyond the drawn line.

Cut ¼" larger than drawn line.

3. Pin or staple the template and the fabric to the placement map on the design wall.

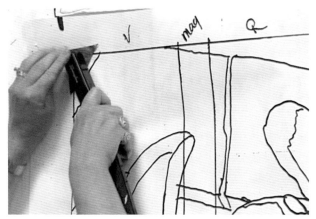

Pin or staple template and fabric to design wall.

4. Cut out all your pieces, and pin or staple them to the design wall.

Assemble the Quilt Top

Checking Fabric Choices

When all of your cutout fabrics are pinned to the wall, make sure all the fabric choices are right before you begin to sew. Look through a reducing glass or the wrong end of a pair of binoculars so you can see what the whole quilt will look like when it is sewn together. If there are fabrics that aren't working because they either demand too much attention, are not strong enough to show off a section, or are the wrong value, change them now. This is easy to do because the template is pinned in place behind the fabric. Remove the pieces that aren't working, and use the template to cut new pieces of fabric.

Machine Piecing

If your pieces are appropriate for machine piecing, follow these steps.

1. Select 2 adjoining pieces, and place them right sides together.

2. Pin the ends to align them. Depending on the length of the seam, you may need to put 1 or 2 pins between the 2 outside pins. Use the drawn lines to make sure the pieces are properly aligned.

3. Sew on the drawn line.

4. Press the seams open to create a smooth line.

5. Continue sewing the pieces together until the quilt top is complete.

Appliqué

If your pieces are appropriate for appliqué, follow these steps.

1. Use the third enlarged pattern copy to trace the design onto stabilizer, which will be used as the foundation for appliqué. I use Sulky Totally Stable, a heat-sensitive iron-on tear-away stabilizer. Draw the lines of the design on the shiny side of the stabilizer with a ballpoint pen. If the design is larger than the stabilizer, fasten several sheets of stabilizer together with small pieces of adhesive tape on the back.

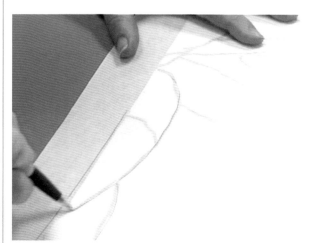

Draw design onto stabilizer.

2. Decide which piece to start with, and remove the appropriate fabric and pattern template from the wall. Use the pattern map to determine which edges of the fabric will lie on top of the adjoining pieces. These top edges will need to be turned.

3. Spray the fabric with spray starch.

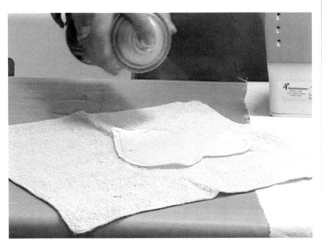

Spray fabric with spray starch.

4. Place the front side of the pattern template in place on the wrong side of the fabric. Turn the edge of the fabric over the template, and iron it in place with the aid of a stiletto. Make sure the spray starch is dry before you remove the template. Press the fabric piece once more to ensure that the edges are flat.

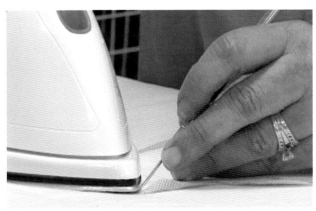

Turn edges of fabric over template for appliqué.

5. Place the fabric piece in position on the stabilizer, using the drawn lines to guide placement. Attach the prepared piece to the stabilizer with the tip of the iron. The pieces that are on top will have turned edges, and the pieces that are underneath will be left flat.

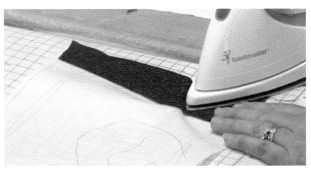

Attach prepared piece to stabilizer.

6. When all the pieces for a section of the quilt are in place, turn the stabilizer over, and press lightly from the back to ensure that all the pieces are attached to the stabilizer and will stay in place. If there are small pieces that do not stick to the stabilizer, glue them in place with a gluestick.

7. Stitch the fabric in place. For hand appliqué, use a blind stitch. For free-motion invisible machine appliqué, use monofilament thread, and set the machine to a zigzag with a stitch width of 2. Stitch around all the edges of the pieces to make sure everything is securely attached.

8. Work in small sections, ironing the pieces to the stabilizer, then sewing them down. Continue this process until all the pieces are in place.

9. Remove the stabilizer when all the pieces have been sewn into place and your quilt top is complete.

Free-Motion Invisible Machine Appliqué

I don't drop the feed dogs (but I do use a darning foot) when I free-motion stitch. I like the extra tension or grip the feed dogs provide, making it easier for me to sew as the fabric doesn't slip as readily. Because the stitching is invisible, my main concern is that all the pieces are securely stitched; I don't worry too much about how each stitch looks. On some machines you do need to drop the feed dogs. If you have the option, experiment and see which works best for you.

Free-motion invisible machine appliqué

Baste

Cut backing fabric and batting 2″ larger all around than the quilt top. Make a quilt sandwich by placing the three layers (backing, batting, and quilt top) in position on a flat surface. Basting holds together the three layers so they can be quilted. The basting can be done by hand with large running stitches, with safety pins, or with a spray-baste adhesive.

Spray Basting

When using spray adhesives, work outside or in a very well-ventilated room.

1. Fold back half of the top layer of the quilt sandwich, and spray the batting with adhesive. Smooth out that half.

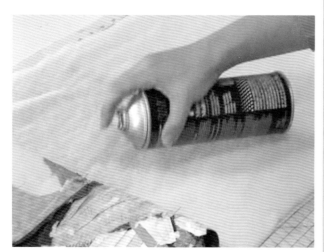

Spray baste half of quilt top.

2. Repeat with the other half.

3. Turn over the quilt sandwich, and follow the same instructions for the backing.

4. Use an iron to press the whole quilt from the back to flatten the batting.

Quilt

Quilting not only holds the layers together; it is an opportunity to enhance your design.

Hand Quilting

For hand quilting, place the basted quilt sandwich in a hoop or a frame, and quilt the layers together with small running stitches. Draw the quilting design on the surface with a fabric-marking pencil, or quilt free-form.

Machine Quilting

You can machine quilt using any method you choose. I prefer free-motion quilting. I use the zigzag setting on my machine, with the stitch width set to 0. This 0 setting will stitch a straight stitch. When I want to create dimension, I adjust the width of the stitch while I am sewing to add a variety of satin-stitch lines where desired.

Sign your name in the lower right-hand corner while machine quilting. I usually just put my first name and the date the quilt was finished.

Finishing

BLOCK THE QUILT

The finished piece must be square or true to the shape intended. The quilt should be blocked so it will lie flat.

1. Place the quilt on a flat surface.

2. Steam the entire surface with a steamer. This can be a professional steamer like the ones used to steam clothes in a dress shop, or it can be an iron that has a steam setting. Start in the center, and work out in circles to the outside edge.

3. Let the quilt dry overnight before moving it.

SQUARE THE QUILT

Squaring means trimming the edges of the quilt so the corners are 90°, or true right angles. If your quilt is not meant to be a square or rectangle, trim as needed.

1. Move the blocked quilt to a large rotary cutting mat.

2. Use a T-square to line up the corners, and trim away anything outside the desired edge.

MAKE A SLEEVE

If your quilt is square or rectangular, a simple sleeve running along the top edge, which a rod can be put through, is the easiest way to display a quilt on a wall. If the quilt has irregular edges, rings can be attached so it can be hooked onto nails in the wall.

Follow these steps to make a hanging sleeve.

1. Cut a strip of fabric 9″ wide by the length of the top edge of the quilt.

2. Turn under the 2 short edges so they won't get caught in the binding on the sides of the quilt, and stitch.

3. Fold the sleeve in half, with the right side out, and pin the unturned edges of the sleeve to the top edge of the quilt, matching the raw edges. These edges will be stitched into the binding. Hand stitch the other side.

4. Hand stitch the folded edge to the back of the quilt.

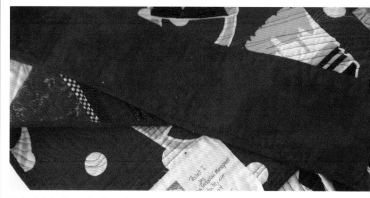

Make fabric sleeve for hanging.

MAKE A LABEL

Use your inspiration photo or painting to create a label. If you are comfortable using a computer, there are many ways to print on fabric using an inkjet printer. The following is another way to create a label.

1. Place the inspiration onto a piece of white paper.

2. Write the quilt title, the size, the date it was completed, and your name, city, and state on the paper.

3. Transfer the image to white fabric using a photo transfer technique. You may have to reduce the image when transferring it to make the label a manageable size.

4. Pin the label to the lower right-hand side of the back of the quilt. The outer edges will be stitched into the binding. Hand stitch the remaining edges of the label.

Create fabric label.

BIND THE QUILT

Binding will finish the raw outside edge of the quilt.

1. Cut fabric on the bias in 1¾"-wide strips.

2. Sew these lengths end-to-end on the diagonal until the strip is long enough to go around the outside edge of the quilt, with some extra for turning corners.

3. Press the strip in half lengthwise, right side out. Machine sew the raw edges to the front of the quilt, right sides together, stitching through the sleeve and the label.

4. Roll the folded edge of the binding to the back of the quilt, and blind stitch in place by hand.

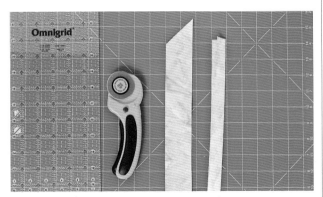

Binding

Print Your Own Labels

You can print your own labels using an inkjet printer and TAP (Transfer Artist Paper) or pretreated fabric sheets. Just follow the instructions on the packages.

DOCUMENT THE QUILT

The final stage of the process is to document all that you have done. This is especially important if you plan to enter your art quilt into a competition.

1. Have the finished quilt photographed by a professional. You may wish to have slides, a 4" × 5" transparency, and digital images. Have digital images made in .jpg versions for emailing and .tifs for reproduction in print.

2. Keep a file of your work that includes the date you finished the quilt, the size, and the title. Keep notes on the techniques used and your inspiration. This will make it easy to fill out forms and answer requests when entering your work in shows or for publication.

Photography Permissions

Even if you don't know how the photography of your finished quilt might be used, be sure to get a signed statement from the photographer giving you the right to use the images as you choose, including submitting them for publication. Unless you do this, and have the statement in writing, the photographer legally owns the copyright to the photographic images.

You are done! Hang your quilt on the wall and enjoy your accomplishment.

Congratulations!

about the author

Fiber artist Katie Pasquini Masopust has traveled throughout the United States and to Canada, New Zealand, Australia, Japan, Belgium, Switzerland, Norway, Denmark, and England teaching contemporary quilt design. She has changed her style several times over the years. After starting with traditional works, she next turned to creating mandalas, followed by dimensional quilts. She then moved on to landscapes, fracturing them and adding transparencies and color washes. Her most recent work is based on her acrylic paintings. She feels that she has come full circle, returning to her beginnings as a painter, but painting now with fabric. Katie teaches in a relaxed but energizing style, passing her extensive knowledge of design and the art quilt on to her students.

Katie has won many awards throughout her career, including receiving the Silver Star Award at the International Quilt Festival in Houston.

Visit Katie's website at www.katiepm.com.

ALSO BY KATIE PASQUINI MASOPUST

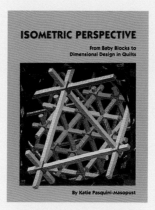

Great Titles *from* C&T PUBLISHING

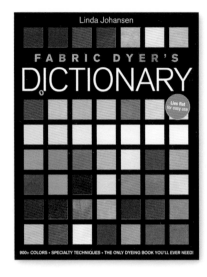

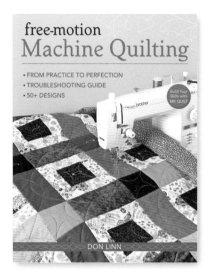

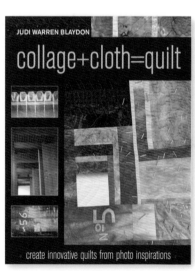

Available at your local retailer or **www.ctpub.com** *or* **800-284-1114**

For a list of other fine books from C&T Publishing, visit our website to view our catalog online.

C&T PUBLISHING, INC.
P.O. Box 1456
Lafayette, CA 94549
800-284-1114

Email: ctinfo@ctpub.com
Website: www.ctpub.com

C&T Publishing's professional photography services are now available to the public. Visit us at www.ctmediaservices.com.

Tips and Techniques can be found at www.ctpub.com > Consumer Resources > Quiltmaking Basics: Tips & Techniques for Quiltmaking & More

For quilting supplies:

COTTON PATCH
1025 Brown Ave.
Lafayette, CA 94549
Store: 925-284-1177
Mail order: 925-283-7883

Email: CottonPa@aol.com
Website: www.quiltusa.com

Note: Fabrics used in the quilts shown may not be currently available, as fabric manufacturers keep most fabrics in print for only a short time.